Thomas Witherow

Which is the Apostolic Church?

An Inquiry at the Oracles of God as to Whether Any Existing form of ...

Thomas Witherow

Which is the Apostolic Church?
An Inquiry at the Oracles of God as to Whether Any Existing form of ...

ISBN/EAN: 9783337064006

Printed in Europe, USA, Canada, Australia, Japan

Cover: Foto ©Lupo / pixelio.de

More available books at **www.hansebooks.com**

WHICH IS THE APOSTOLIC CHURCH?

AN INQUIRY

AT THE ORACLES OF GOD AS TO WHETHER ANY EXISTING FORM OF CHURCH GOVERNMENT IS OF DIVINE RIGHT.

BY

THOMAS WITHEROW,
PROFESSOR OF CHURCH HISTORY, LONDONDERRY, IRELAND.

EDITED AND ANNOTATED

BY THE

Rev. R. M. PATTERSON.

PHILADELPHIA:
PRESBYTERIAN BOARD OF PUBLICATION,
1334 CHESTNUT STREET.

CONTENTS.

	PAGE
STATEMENT OF THE QUESTION	5
Meaning of the word Church	19
Government of the Church	30
APOSTOLIC PRINCIPLES	42
The First Principle	46
The Second Principle	55
The Third Principle	62
The Fourth Principle	68
The Fifth Principle	73
The Sixth Principle	84
APPLICATION OF THE TEST	91
Prelacy	93
Independency	100
Presbytery	109
The Result	117

PREFATORY NOTE.

This little book of Professor Witherow, of Londonderry, is an admirably compact, clean-cut and forcible inquiry into the great principles and facts of church government. It is well adapted to strengthen the faith of Presbyterians in their system, and to convince candid inquirers of its apostolic character. As originally published in Ireland, it contained references to the Presbyterians of that country which would not apply to American Presbyterians in general. Its descriptions of the antagonistic forms of ecclesiastical government were also somewhat colored by and restricted to the British organizations. In order to prepare this edition for American readers (at the request of the Board of Publication), the first class of passages have been eliminated, and the second have been supplemented by foot-notes characterizing some of the leading ecclesiastical organizations of this country, and showing the application to them of the principles that are laid down in the text. These changes have been made with the courteous consent of Professor Witherow. The title of the Irish edition of the book was: "The Apostolic Church: Which is it?" In this edition a transposition of the words of that title has been made, because the Board of Publication has already on its catalogue a work on the same subject, by the Rev. Albert Barnes, with the title, "The Apostolic Church."

We have endeavored not to multiply the notes, but to restrict them to the smallest possible number and compass, so as to keep the book small in size.

R. M. P.

WHICH IS THE APOSTOLIC CHURCH?

STATEMENT OF THE QUESTION.

IT is very common for professing Christians to draw a distinction between *essentials* and *non-essentials* in religion, and to infer that if any fact or doctrine rightly belongs to the latter class it must be a matter of very little importance, and may in practice be safely set at naught. The great bulk of men take their opinions on trust; they will not undergo the toil of thinking, searching and reasoning about anything, and one of the most usual expedients adopted to save them the trouble of inquiry, and to turn aside the force of any disagreeable fact, is to meet it by saying, "The matter is not essential to salvation;

therefore we need give ourselves little concern on the subject."

If the distinction here specified is safe, the inference drawn from it is certainly dangerous. To say that because a fact of divine revelation is not essential to salvation it must of necessity be unimportant, and may or may not be received by us, is to assert a principle the application of which would make havoc of our Christianity. For what are truths essential to salvation? Are they not these: That there is a God; that all men are sinners; that the Son of God died upon the cross to make atonement for the guilty; and that whosoever believes on the Lord Jesus Christ shall be saved? There is good reason for believing that not a few souls are now in happiness who in life knew little more than these, the first principles of the oracles of God—the very alphabet of the Christian system; and if so, no other divine truths can be counted absolutely essential to salvation. But if all the other truths of revelation are unimportant because they happen to be non-essentials, it follows that the word of God itself is in the main unimportant; for by far the greatest portion of it is occupied with matters the knowledge of which, in the case supposed, is not absolutely indispensable to the everlasting happiness of men. Nor does it alter the case if we regard the number of fundamental truths to be much greater. Let a man once persuade himself that importance attaches only to what he is pleased to call essentials, whatever their number, and he will, no doubt, shorten his creed and cut away the foundation of many controversies, but he will practically set aside all except a very small part of the Scriptures. If such a principle does not mutilate the Bible, it stigmatizes much of it as trivial. Revelation is all gold for preciousness and purity, but the very touch of such a principle would transmute the most of it into dross.

Though every statement in the Scriptures cannot be regarded as absolutely essential to salvation, yet everything there is essential to some other wise and important end, else it would not find a place in the good word of God. Human wisdom may be baffled in attempting to specify the design of every truth that forms a component part of divine revelation, but eternity will show us that no portion of it is useless. All Scripture is profitable. A fact written therein may not be essential to human salvation, and yet it may be highly conducive to some other great and gracious purpose in the economy of God—it may be necessary for our personal comfort, for our guidance in life or for our growth in holiness, and most certainly it is essential to the completeness of the system of divine truth. The law of the Lord is perfect. Strike out of the Bible the truth that seems the most insignificant of all, and the law of the Lord would not be perfect any more. In architecture, the pinning that fills a crevice in the wall occupies a subordinate position, in comparison with the quoin; but the builder lets us know that the one has an important purpose to serve as well as the other, and does its part to promote the stability and completeness of the house. In shipbuilding, the screws and bolts that gird the ship together are insignificant, as compared with the beams of oak and masts of

STATEMENT OF THE QUESTION. 9

pine, but they contribute their full share to the safety of the vessel and the security of the passenger. So in the Christian system every fact, great or small, that God has been pleased to insert in the Bible, is, by its very position, invested with importance, answers its end, and, though perhaps justly considered as non-essential to salvation, does not deserve to be accounted as worthless.

Every divine truth is important, though it may be that all divine truths are not of equal importance. The simplest statement of the Bible is a matter of more concern to an immortal being than the most sublime sentiment of mere human genius. The one carries with it what the other cannot show—the stamp of the approval of God. The one comes to us from heaven; the other savors of the earth. The one has for us a special interest, as forming a constituent portion of that word which is a message from God to each individual man; the other is the production of a mind merely human, to which we and all our interests were alike unknown. Any truth merely human should weigh with us light as a feather in comparison with the most insignificant of the truths of God. The faith of a Christian should strive to reach and grasp everything that God has honored with a place in that word the design of which is to be a light to our feet as we thread our way through this dark world. Besides, this, unlike every other book, is not doomed to perish. Heaven and earth may pass away, but the words of Christ shall not pass away. The seal of eternity is stamped on every verse of the Bible. This fact is enough of itself to make every line of it important.

With these observations we deem it right to introduce our exposition of ecclesiastical polity. Few would go so far as to assert that correct views on church government are essential to salvation, and yet it is a subject whose importance it were folly to attempt to depreciate. The Holy Spirit, speaking in the Scriptures, treats of this theme. The Christian world has been divided in opinion about it ever since the Reformation. We cannot attach ourselves to any denomination of Christians without giving our influence either to truth or error on this very point; and the views we adopt upon this subject go far to color our opinions on matters of Christian faith and practice. With such facts before us, though we may not regard the polity of the New Testament Church as essential to human salvation, we do not feel at liberty to undervalue its importance.

The various forms of Church government that we find existing at present in the Christian world may be classed under some one or other of these heads: PRELACY, INDEPENDENCY and PRESBYTERY. We do not employ these terms in an offensive sense, but as being the best calculated to denote their respective systems. *Prelacy* is that form of Church government which is administered by archbishops, bishops, deans, archdeacons and other ecclesiastical office-bearers, depending on their hierarchy, and is such as we see exemplified in the Greek Church, the Church of Rome and the Church of England.* *In-*

* A more minute definition of Prelacy is given by Principal Hill in his "Lectures in Divinity," p. 719 (Carter's edition): "There is in the Church a superior

dependency is that form of Church government whose distinctive principle is that each order of office-bearers, the successors of the apostles, who possess in their own persons the right of ordination and jurisdiction, and who are called ἐπίσκοποι, as being the overseers not only of the people, but also of the clergy, and an inferior order of ministers, called presbyters, the literal translation of the word πρεσβύτεροι, which is rendered in our English Bible elders, persons who receive, from the ordination of the bishop, power to preach and to administer the sacraments, who are set over the people, but are themselves under the government of the bishop, and have no right to convey to others the sacred office which he gives them authority to exercise under him." In other words, "the prelatical theory assumes the perpetuity of the apostleship as the governing power in the Church, which, therefore, consists of those who profess the true religion and are subject to apostle-bishops. This is the Anglican or High Church form of this theory. In its Low Church form, the prelatical theory simply teaches that there was originally a threefold order in the ministry, and that there should be now." (Dr. Hodge, "What is Presbyterianism?" p. 5.) The papal form adds to the theory the ideas that Peter was the primate of the apostles, that the bishop of Rome, as his successor, is primate over the apostle-bishops, and that it is essential to the Church to have "a vicar of Christ, a perpetual college of apostles, and the people subject to their infallible control." Three orders in the ministry—deacons, priests and bishops—the last named separate congregation is under Christ subject to no external jurisdiction whatever, but has within itself—in its office-bearers and members—all the materials of government, and is such as is at present in practical operation among Congregationalists and Baptists. *Presbytery* is that form of Church government which is dispensed by presbyters or elders, met in session, presbytery, synod, or general assembly; and is such as is presented in the several Presbyterian Churches of Ireland, Scotland, England and America. These three forms of ecclesiastical polity are at this moment extensively prevalent in Christendom. Indeed, every other organization that any considerable body of Christians has adopted is only a modification or a mixture of some of the systems we have named.*

of whom are the successors of the apostles and the rulers of all: this is the one principle which runs through all the varied and varying forms of prelacy.

P.

* The Methodist Episcopal Church, for instance, in its government is a mixture of Episcopacy and Presbyterianism. It recognizes two *offices* which are also *orders* in the ministry—that of deacons, who are preaching min-

A very brief examination enables us to see that these three systems differ very widely in their characteristic features. Not only so, but Prelacy, in all its main principles, is opposed to Presbytery; and Independency, in its main principles, is opposed to both. It follows that three forms differing so very much cannot all be right, and cannot, of course, have equal claims on the attachment and support of enlightened and conscientious men. It is self-evident, moreover, that the word of God, the only rule of faith and practice, cannot approve of all; for as the word of God never contradicts itself, it cannot sanction contradictory systems. Some one of the three must be more in accordance with the will of God, as expressed in the Scriptures, than either of the

---

isters, and that of presbyters or elders, who are a higher order of the ministry, and to whom alone belong the powers of government and of ordination. It also possesses a third *office*, that of bishop or general superintendent, which in *order* is Presbyterial, but in *office* Episcopal. (Hawley's "Manual of Methodism," pp. 144–150.) But none of these officers is chosen by the people. There is not a plurality of elders in each church; not are the conferences church courts of review and appeal. P.

others, and to know which of them is so should be a subject of deep interest to every child of God. A Christian, of all men, is bound to be a lover of the truth; and we are warranted in supposing that if a Christian could only see to which of these competing systems the word of truth bears witness, he would support it with all his might, and would lend no encouragement to the others. If a man, after he sees the difference, can hold what he knows to be merely human in the same estimation with what he knows to be divine, let him bid farewell to his Christianity, and cease to pretend that he cherishes any attachment to the truth. The religion of the Lord Jesus, unless we greatly mistake its spirit, binds all who receive it to prefer the true to the false, the right to the wrong, the good to the evil; and for us to be tempted by any consideration to hold them in equal reverence and render them equal support is to fling one of the first requirements of Christianity away from us. The influence of a Christian is often very little in this world; but whatever it is, it is a talent, for which, like his time, his money or his intellectual power, he is accountable to God, and that influence ought ever to be on the side of the truth, never against the truth.

Which, then, of the three forms of Church government prevalent throughout the world is it the duty of a Christian to select and to support?

This question must be decided by the standard of the word of God. That book is quite sufficient to point out the path of duty in this as well as in all other matters, for it was intended by its divine Author to be our guide in matters of practice as well as of faith. The Bible furnishes us with peculiar facilities for forming an opinion on this very point. It tells us of a Church that was organized in the world eighteen hundred years ago. The founders of that Church were apostles and prophets, acting by the authority of God. Every fact known with certainty about the original constitution of the Church is preserved in the Bible; everything preserved elsewhere is only hearsay and tradition. We read in Scripture very many facts that enable us to know with tolerable accuracy the history, doctrine, worship and government of that Church which existed in apostolic days. The principles of government set up in a Church which was founded by inspired men must have had, we are sure, the approbation of God. Corruptions in government as well as in doctrine sprang up at a very early period, but the Church in apostolic days was purer in those aspects than it ever has been in subsequent times. The most obvious method, therefore, of arriving at the truth is to compare our modern systems of ecclesiastical government with the model presented in the holy Scriptures. That which bears the closest resemblance to the divine original is most likely itself to be divine.

The warmest friends of existing ecclesiastical systems cannot fairly object to such a test. There is scarcely a Church on earth that is not loud in its pretensions to apostolicity. The Prelatic Churches claim to be apostolic. The Independent Churches claim to be apostolic. The Presbyterian Churches claim to be apostolic. Each of these denominations professes to maintain the same doctrine, worship and government that distinguished the Church which was planted by the apostles of the Lord. On one of these points—that of ecclesiastical government—we propose to examine these claims by the very test that themselves have chosen. Divesting ourselves of all prejudice, we come to the law and to the testimony, desirous to know what God says on the topic in question, and determined to follow where the Scripture points, let that be where it may. Let us search the Bible, to see what it teaches on this great theme. If, on a thorough examination, we fail to discover there any clear and definite principles of Church government, the conclusion of necessity follows that Prelacy, Independency, and Presbytery are upon a level—none of them is based upon divine authority—and it becomes a matter of mere expediency and convenience which form we support. If we find, on the other hand, that certain great principles of Church government are embodied in the Scriptures, then, when we have ascertained accurately what these principles are, we have reached the mind of God upon the matter, and we have discovered a touch-stone wherewith we can try the value of existing systems, and determine how much is human and how much divine in every one of them.

MEANING OF THE WORD CHURCH.

The word *Church* in our common discourse is used in a variety of senses. Sometimes it signifies the material building erected for divine worship; sometimes it means the people usually assembling in such a building; sometimes the aggregate body of the clergy as distinguished from the laity; sometimes the collective body of professing Christians. As general use is the law of language, it does not become us to take exception to the variety of significations that are given to the term by our best writers, nor can we even say that much practical inconvenience arises from them, inasmuch as the accompanying circumstances usually determine the specific sense in which the word is to be understood. But it is never to be forgotten that when we come to the interpretation of the word of God, the variety of senses commonly attached to the term is altogether inadmissible, and would, if adopted, darken and corrupt the meaning of divine revelation. The word Church in Scripture has always one meaning, and only one—*an assembly of the people of God—a society of Christians.* The Greek word *ecclesia*, in its primary and civil sense, means any assembly called together for any purpose (Acts xix. 32); but in its appropriated and religious sense, it means *a society of Christians,* and is invariably translated by the word *Church.* Examine the Scriptures from the commencement to the close, and you will find that the word Church never has any other meaning but that which we have stated. Let any man who feels disposed to dispute this statement produce, if he can, any passage from the word of God where the sense would be impaired, if the phrase *society of Christians* or *Christian assembly* were substituted for the word Church. This, we are persuaded, would be impossible.

Though the meaning of the word *Church* is in Scripture always the same, let it be observed that its applications are various. It is applied, at the pleasure of the writer, to any society of Christians, however great or however small. Examples of this fact will not fail to suggest themselves to all who are familiar with the word of God. We give a few passages as specimens:

Col. iv. 15. "Salute the brethren which are in Laodicea, and Nymphas, and the Church which is in his house." There the term is applied to a *society of Christians* so small as to be able to find accommodations in a private dwelling-house.

Acts xi. 22. "Then tidings of these things came unto the ears of the Church which was in Jerusalem." There it means a *society of Christians* residing in the same city, and including, as we know on excellent authority, several thousand persons.

Acts vii. 38. "This is he (Moses) that was in the Church in the wilderness with the angel which spake to him in Mount Sinai, and with our fathers: who received the lively oracles to give unto us." Here the word signifies a *society of Christians*—an assembly of God's people so large as to include a whole nation, consisting at the time of at least two millions in number. The term is also applied to the people of God in the days of David, when residing in Canaan, spread over a great extent of territory, and amounting to many millions. Heb. ii. 12, compared with Psalm xxii. 22–25.

1 Cor. xii. 28. "And God hath set some in the Church, first, apostles; secondarily, prophets; thirdly, teachers; after that miracles; then gifts of healings, helps, governments, diversities of tongues." Here the term means the *society of Christians* residing on earth; for it was among them, not among the saints in glory, that God raised up men endowed with apostolic and prophetical gifts.

Eph. v. 25. "Husbands, love your wives, even as Christ also loved the Church, and gave himself for it." The word is here used to signify the *society of Christians* in the largest sense—all for whom Christ died—the whole family of God—all saints in heaven and all believers on earth, viewed as one great company.

STATEMENT OF THE QUESTION.   23

Let it be observed, however, that, amid all this variety of application, the word Church never alters its sense. Its meaning in every occurrence is the same. However applied, it never ceases to signify a *society of Christians;* but whether the society that the inspired writer has in view is great or small, general or particular, is to be learned, not from the term, but from the circumstances in which the term is used. In every instance it is from the context, never from the word itself, that we are to gather whether the society of Christians intended by the writer is to be understood of the collective company of God's people in heaven and earth, or only of those on the earth, in a nation, in a city or in a private house. The practice—into which the best expositors of the Scriptures are occasionally betrayed—of taking up some idea conveyed by the context only, and regarding that idea as entering into the meaning of some particular word, has been shown by a late eminent critic to be the origin of those numerous significations—perplexing by their very multitude—appended almost to every word in our classical dictionaries, and the prolific source of errors in the interpretation of the word of God. This is obviously what has led many to suppose that the word Church has two meanings, signifying something different when referring to the universal body of believers from what it does when denoting the body of believers connected with a particular locality. The truth is that the word Church has only one meaning, but it has a variety of applications. The term of itself never conveys any idea but a society of Christians; it is the context that invariably determines its general or particular application. It is manifestly inaccurate, therefore, to maintain that an idea, invariably conveyed by the context, enters into the meaning of the term, when, as all must admit, the term, apart from the context, does not suggest either a limited or universal application.

Had we occasion to speak of the several Christian congregations of a province or nation in their separate capacity, it would be quite in accordance with the scriptural idiom to designate them the *Churches* of that region.

None can forget how frequently the apostle speaks of the Churches of Syria and Achaia, Galatia and Asia. So, if we required to speak of the individual congregations of Christians in Ireland—the separate Christian societies scattered over the country—we might denominate them the Churches of Ireland, there being nothing in existing ecclesiastical usages to make such language either unintelligible or liable to be misunderstood. But it deserves to be noticed that when we use such phrases as the "Established Church of Scotland," the "Episcopal Church of America" or the "Presbyterian Church of Ireland," there is no departure whatever from the scriptural sense of the word. The meaning of the word in Scripture, as we have seen, invariably is a society of Christians, and this is precisely its meaning in any of the above phrases, the context, at the same time, limiting the Christians in question to those professing certain principles and belonging to a particular country. When we employ, for instance, such a designation as the *Presbyterian Church of Ireland*, the word Church is used precisely in the scriptural sense, to denote a society of Christians, which we learn from the context professes Presbyterian principles and resides in Ireland.

The propriety of applying the term to signify the Christian people of a country does not arise from the fact that they are ever assembled in one congregation, either personally or by representatives, but from the fact that the mind contemplates them as a collective body. All saints in heaven and believers on earth are styled the *Church,* not because they are assembled either literally or figuratively, but because, in the view of the mind, they are regarded as a great society, separated from the world, and united by common principles into one great brotherhood. And so the Christians of any denomination, though composing a multitude of congregations, may, in their aggregate capacity, be properly styled a Church, not because they are either figuratively or literally assembled, but because, in the view of the mind, they are regarded as a collective body, distinguished from others, and united among themselves, by the profession of a common creed.

It was once doubted whether the Scriptures contain an example of the word Church being applied to the Christians of a *country*. The science of biblical criticism has now set that question at rest. The true reading of Acts ix. 31 is, "Then had the *Church* rest throughout all Judea, and Galilee, and Samaria; and walking in the fear of the Lord, and in the comfort of the Holy Ghost, *was* multiplied." No man with the slightest pretensions to scholarship can now hesitate about receiving this as the original form of the text, when it is known that the lately discovered MS.—the *Codex Sinaiticus*—is in its favor, no less than A, B, C, these four being at once the most ancient and valuable manuscripts of the New Testament now extant.* Not to

* The ancient MSS. of the Greek Testament which are still in existence, and to which critics appeal for the settlement of the inspired text, are, as a matter of convenience and for the sake of easy reference, designated by alphabetical letters. The one marked A was probably written in the first half of the fifth century. It was presented to the English Charles I. in 1628 by the patriarch

speak of the evidence derivable from versions and Fathers, the united voices of these four MSS. is enough to settle the correct form of any text: their testimony as to the original reading of Acts ix. 31 none can question; and to that passage we confidently point as a clear instance of the word *Church* being applied to the Christians of a country, viewed as one collective society, though in reality divided into many separate congregations.

Some writers, indeed, give a different account of the matter. They tell us that the

---

of Constantinople, and is preserved in the British Museum. It contains the whole Greek Bible, with a few chasms in the New Testament. B is also a MS. of the whole Greek Bible. It belongs to the fourth century, and since 1450 has been in the Vatican Library. C was written in the fifth century, and is now in the Royal Library at Paris. It contains fragments of the Greek Old Testament, and of every part of the New Testament. The *Codex Sinaiticus* (also marked ℵ) is the oldest MS. of the New Testament that is known to be in existence. It probably belongs to the fourth century, and is complete. The celebrated Russian critic, Tischendorf, found it in 1859 in the convent of St. Catherine on Mt. Sinai; hence its title. This is the one which is referred to in the text. P.

universal community of Christians in heaven and on earth is called in Scripture the *Church,* not because they are viewed as one great brotherhood, united by common principles, but because they "are at all times truly and properly assembled in Jesus." It is a mere fancy to suppose that the mind ever takes such a fact into account when employing the term in its universal application; but if so, it does not alter the case. The Christians of a particular district, or of a province, or of a nation, may be properly designated a Church for the same reasons, because they also "are at all times truly and properly assembled in Jesus." There is no sense in which all the Christians on earth and in heaven are "assembled in Jesus" that the Christians of any particular country are not thus assembled. If the whole is assembled, so also are the parts. Take the matter either way, the Christians of a district, or a province, or a kingdom, holding certain principles in common, if viewed as a collective community, are a Church, exactly in the sense of the Scriptures. They are a Society of Christians.

GOVERNMENT OF THE CHURCH.

The Christian society on earth, or, as it is usually called, the Church, is represented in the Scriptures as a *kingdom*. It was of his Church that the Lord Jesus spake when he said to Pilate, "My kingdom is not of this world." John xviii. 36. The fact of its being a kingdom necessarily implies at least three things—first, a *king* or governor; secondly, *subjects;* thirdly, *laws*. In the Church or kingdom of God, the king is *Christ;* the subjects are *believers* and their children; the laws are the *Scriptures* of truth.

Every king has officers under him who are charged with the execution of his laws, and who have authority from the crown to do justice and judgment. Judges and magistrates are the office-bearers of a kingdom, deriving their power from the monarch under whom they serve, and putting the laws in force among all ranks and classes of the people. Hence a very palpable division of a kingdom is into *rulers* and *ruled*—those whose duty is to administer the law, and those who are

STATEMENT OF THE QUESTION. 31

bound to obey it. The same distinction holds in the kingdom of Christ. It also consists of rulers and ruled—the office-bearers entrusted with the dispensation of the laws, and the people who are commanded to yield them submission. This is very plain, from Heb. xiii. 17: "Obey them that have the rule over you, and submit yourselves: for they watch for your souls, as they that must give account." It is clear from this passage that there are some in the Church whose duty it is to rule; they are the office-bearers of the Church. It is no less clear that there are others in the Church whose duty is to obey; they are the private members—the subjects of the kingdom—the people.

But in every society where it is the acknowledged duty of some parties to exercise authority, and of others to practice submission, there must be what is called *government;* for in such authority exercised on the one hand, and in such submission rendered on the other, the essence of all government consists. Even were there no passage in the Scriptures but that last quoted bearing upon the subject, it is undeniable that government was established in the apostolic Church. If government existed, some *form* of government must have been adopted; for to say there was established in the kingdom of Christ government without a form of government is absurd. History tells us of many ecclesiastical and political wonders; but of all the strange things that have been witnessed in the world or in the Church since the beginning of time, there has never yet appeared government without a form of government. The thing is impossible. Government in itself is an abstraction. The moment it puts forth power, it becomes a reality—it stands before the world a visible thing—it assumes a form.

That there was government in the apostolic Church, and that this government existed under a certain form, seems clear to demonstration. To determine with precision what this form was is a matter of great consequence, for it must be evident to all that a plan of Church government, instituted by the apostles of the Lord, acting under the guidance of the Holy Spirit, must carry with it a degree of lawfulness and authority that no human system, though in itself a master-piece of wisdom—made venerable by age, or recommended by expediency—ever can exhibit; and that every form of Church government is deserving of respect only so far as it conforms in its principles to that divine original. But there are obvious reasons that make it a matter of some difficulty to ascertain with accuracy the system of ecclesiastical polity that was established in the New Testament Church.

1. The apostles, writing to Christians who were themselves members of the apostolic Church, and of course well acquainted with its organization, did not judge it necessary to enter into detailed description of the Christian society. To do so would have been unnatural. They do occasionally state facts bearing on Church government, and hint indirectly at prevailing practices. These hints and facts were sufficiently suggestive and intelligible to the persons originally addressed, but by us, who live in a distant age, in a foreign country and among associations

widely different, they are not so easily understood.

2. They do not even arrange such facts as bear upon the question in systematic order. If man had had the making of the Bible, it would have been a very different book; but as that circumstance was not left to our option, we must take it as we find it. On examination, we see that it teaches nothing in scientific order. Even morality and doctrine are not there arranged in regular system, but are conveyed in detached portions, and our industry is stimulated by having to gather the scattered fragments, to compare them with each other, and to work them up into order for ourselves. So ecclesiastical polity is not taught in Scripture methodically; but away over the wide field of revelation, facts and hints and circumstances lie scattered, which we are to search for, and examine, and combine, and classify. Now, all do not agree in the arrangement of these facts, nor in the inferences that legitimately flow from them, nor in the mode of constructing a system from the detached material.

STATEMENT OF THE QUESTION. 35

These things make it difficult to ascertain with accuracy, and still more so, with unanimity, the form of Church government that existed in apostolic days.* But difficult as it

---

* A chief reason why the principles of government are not prescribed at length and in a formal way in the New Testament is this: While the Church of God was reorganized after the ascension of our Lord, it remained essentially the same with the Old Testament body; and when its separate organization took place, it was on the ancient model. The Eldership existed in the Jewish Church, and is the permanent essential office of the organization under both dispensations. Hence, the creation of it is nowhere recorded in the New Testament, as in the case of deacons and apostles, because the latter were created to meet new and special exigencies, while the former was transmitted from the earliest times. (See Dr. J. A. Alexander's Primitive Church Officers, p. 28.) Archbishop Whately says "it is likely that several of the earliest Christian churches were converted synagogues, which became Christian churches as soon as the members, or as soon as the main part of their members, acknowledged Jesus as the Messiah." In such cases, he says, "the apostles did not there so much form a Christian church (or congregation, *ecclesia*) as make an existing congregation Christian by introducing the Christian sacraments and worship, and establishing whatever regulations were necessary for the newly adopted faith, leaving the machinery (if I may so speak) of government unchanged, the rulers of syna-

seems, it is proved quite possible, by a thorough and unprejudiced examination of the Scriptures, to discover the main principles that entered into the constitution of the primitive Church. We say the *main principles*—more than these we need not expect to find. The word of God, except in some rare instances, never enters into details—it states principles.

This is a very noticeable peculiarity of the divine legislation that deserves a passing remark. In every civilized country it may be observed how those entrusted with the duty of government aim to provide a law for every specific case. The human legislator descends to details. The result of this in our

gogues, elders and other officers (whether spiritual or ecclesiastical, or both) being already provided for in the existing institutions." ("The Kingdom of Christ Delineated," pp. 84-86.) Hence, as the church-membership of the children of believers is not formally commanded in the New Testament, because it already existed, so the permanent governmental principles of the Church are not explicitly enunciated, because they were already existing as facts. In both cases unrepealed laws are implied in the New Testament history, and instances of obedience to them in the apostolic Church are given for our guidance.   P.

STATEMENT OF THE QUESTION. 37

own country is that the common and statute laws of England are so bulky that the books in which they are written would make of themselves a magnificent library. Parliament meets every year for the express purpose of constructing new and amending old laws, to suit the ever-varying circumstances of the country and the times; and notwithstanding all, cases occur daily in the public courts wherein the most accomplished jurists have to acknowledge that the existing laws determine nothing. But observe how the divine law proceeds on a method quite different. It rarely enters into specific details, but lays down general principles any one of which is quite sufficient to decide a whole multitude of cases. Instead, for instance, of attempting to prescribe every form of good that it is right for a man to perform to his neighbor, it lays down a principle quite sufficient to meet every case—Thou shalt love thy neighbor as thyself. Instead of enumerating the different ways by which children are to discharge the duties that they owe their parents, Scripture enacts this general law, holding good in every case—Honor thy father and thy mother. Declining to specify every semblance of sin that it were well for Christians to avoid, the statutes of the Lord direct us to —Abstain from all appearance of evil. Human legislation enters into minute details, but divine legislation enacts general principles. The result is that while there is perhaps more room left for difference of opinion in the interpretation and application of the enactments of a code of law constructed on the latter system, yet this disadvantage is more than counterbalanced by the fact that the laws of God are in themselves perfect; that they do not change with the ever varying circumstances of countries and of times; that they meet every case which can possibly occur; and that they are compressed into a reasonable size, being all written in a book so small that it can be lifted in the hand or carried in the pocket. Now, the Scripture teaches us Church government as it teaches morality. It does not furnish minute details, but it supplies THE GREAT LIVING PRINCIPLES that entered into the polity of the Apostolic

Church. What these main principles were it is now our purpose to ascertain.*

It is the common practice of writers, in discussing the important subject of ecclesiastical government, to select some one of our modern churches which happens to be a favorite, delineate its characteristic features, and then proceed to show that they are a reflection of the pattern presented in the word of God. That this plan has some recommendations we can readily believe, but it is no less obvious that it is liable to grave objections. It seems to assume at the commencement the conclusion to which the reasoner can only hope to conduct us after a sound process of logic. It somehow produces the fatal impression that the writer has determined in the first place that his view of the subject is right, and then goes to Scripture to search for proof of it. The author may be the most impartial and truth-loving of men, but his very plan betrays a preference for some particular system, and thus, at the

* This paragraph was suggested by reading Dr. Paley's Sermon on Rom. xiv. 7, p. 521.

outset, awakes the prejudices of many readers. Besides, it affords opportunities for viewing passages of Scripture apart from their connection, and tempts writers to quote their favorite texts, the sound of which only is upon their side. For these reasons we do not choose to adopt this method on the present occasion.

The plan of procedure we propose is more unusual, though, we trust, not less satisfactory. We will examine the Holy Scriptures with a view of ascertaining from them the various facts that bear on the government of the apostolic Church. We will produce the passages, contemplate them in their immediate connection, unfold their meaning, and try if by their aid we can arrive at GREAT PRINCIPLES. We will then turn to our modern Churches, view the different forms of ecclesiastical polity that exist in the world at present, and see which of them it is that embodies all or most of these principles. When this is done, we shall have found the denomination that, in point of government, is best entitled to be regarded as the *apostolic Church*.

This process of reasoning is so very clear and simple that there is no room for practicing deception either on ourselves or our readers. The very humblest intellect may follow our logic to the close. There are but two steps until we arrive at the conclusion:

First, we are to ascertain from the unerring word of God what were the main principles in the government of the churches founded by the apostles of the Lord; 'and, *secondly*, we are to ascertain in which of our modern Churches these main principles are most fully acknowledged and carried out.

We will then apply to the settlement of the matter an axiom radiant in the light of its own self-evidence. That axiom is, THE MODERN CHURCH WHICH EMBODIES IN ITS GOVERNMENT MOST APOSTOLIC PRINCIPLES COMES NEAREST IN ITS GOVERNMENT TO THE APOSTOLIC CHURCH.

APOSTOLIC PRINCIPLES.

FROM a careful examination of the Scripture, we find at least four different kinds of office-bearers in the apostolic Church—1. Apostles. 2. Evangelists. 3. Bishops, also called pastors and teachers. 4. Deacons. Each one of these had a right to exercise all the offices inferior to his own, but one filling an inferior had no right to discharge the duties of a superior office. Thus, the apostolic office included all the others, and a bishop or elder had the right to act as a deacon, so long as his doing so did not impede the due discharge of duties peculiarly his own. A deacon, on the other hand, had no right to exercise the office of a bishop, nor had a bishop any authority to take on him the duties of an apostle. Each superior office included all below it.

Two of these offices—those of apostle and evangelist—were temporary, necessary at the first establishment of Christianity, but not necessary to be perpetuated. The *apostles* were witnesses of the resurrection of the Lord Jesus, endowed with the power of working miracles and of conferring the Holy Ghost by the laying on of their hands, the infallible expounders of the divine will and the founders of the Christian Church; and having served the purpose for which they were sent, they disappeared out of the world, and, as apostles, have left no successors. *Evangelists* were missionaries—men who traveled from place to place preaching the gospel, and who acted as the assistants and delegates of the apostles in organizing churches.* Of these, Philip and Timothy and Titus were the most eminent examples. It deserves to be remarked, with regard to these temporary or, as they are usually called, extraordinary office-

* While our Presbyterian "Form of Government" does not, in Ch. III., expressly mention evangelists among "the ordinary and perpetual officers in the church," it does provide, in Ch. XV., an ordination service for such ministers "to preach the gospel, administer sealing ordinances and organize churches in frontier or destitute settlements." In the missionary work of the Church they are still needed and provided for.   P.

bearers, that their sphere of duty was not limited to a congregation, but extended to the Church at large. They were members of any Christian society within whose bounds they resided for a time, but their mission was to the world, and their authority extended to the Church universal.

The offices of *bishop* and *deacon* were, on the other hand, designed to be perpetuated in the Church. The bishops, or, as they are more usually called, elders,* and pastors, and teachers, were office-bearers, whose duty it was to instruct and govern the Church. The deacons had charge of temporal concerns, and were entrusted with the special duty of ministering to the necessities of the poor. The Church can never cease to have need of these two offices, so long as its members have spiritual and temporal wants to be supplied. But it is to be observed, with regard to the bishops and deacons, that they were mainly congregational officers. The sphere of their duty was not so general as that of the apos-

* This is assumed for the present: it will be proved afterward.

tles, prophets and evangelists, but lay for the most part within the bounds of that particular church or district for which they were appointed to act.

Dr. Campbell thus expounds the special necessity that existed in the primitive Church, both for the temporary and perpetual officebearers: "To take a similitude from temporal things: it is one thing to conquer a kingdom and become master of it, and another thing to govern it when conquered so as to retain the possession which has been acquired. The same agents and the same expedients are not properly adapted to both. For the first of these purposes, there was a set of extraordinary ministers or officers in the Church, who, like the military forces intended for conquest, could not be fixed to a particular spot whilst there remained any provinces to conquer. Their charge was, in a manner, universal, and their functions ambulatory. For the second, there was a set of ordinary ministers or pastors, corresponding to civil governors, to whom it was necessary to allot distinct charges or precincts, to which their services were chiefly to be confined, in order to instruct the people, to preside in the public worship and religious ordinances, and to give them the necessary assistance for the regulation of their conduct. Without this second arrangement, the acquisitions made could not have been long retained. There must have ensued a universal relapse into idolatry and infidelity. This distinction of ministers into extraordinary and ordinary has been admitted by controvertists on both sides, and therefore cannot justly be considered as introduced (which sometimes happens to distinctions) to serve a hypothesis."* With these preliminary observations, we proceed in search of—

THE FIRST PRINCIPLE.

All offices in the Christian Church take origin from the Lord Jesus. Himself is the Author and embodiment of them all; he is the Apostle of our profession; he is an Evangelist, preaching peace to them that are afar off, and to them that are nigh; he is the

* Lectures on Ecclesiastical History, Lecture iv., 3d Edition, London, 1824.

APOSTOLIC PRINCIPLES. 47

great Pastor or Shepherd of the sheep—the Bishop of souls; and he is the Deacon or servant who came not to be ministered to, but to minister. All offices in the Church are embodied in the person of Christ.

The apostles were the only office-bearers chosen during the life-time of the Lord. They held their appointments immediately from himself. They were called to the work of the ministry by his voice, and they received their commission at his hands. Simon and Andrew were casting their nets into the Lake of Galilee, as Jesus walked upon the beach, but at his call they left their nets to follow him through the world. The sons of Zebedee heard his voice, and forthwith they forgot both father and mother in their ambition to become fishers of men. When Christ said, "Follow me," Levi forsook the receipt of custom, and was a publican no more. The personal call of the Lord Jesus was then, and is still, the first and best of all authority to hold office in the Church of God. Let a man only satisfy us that he holds his appointment directly from the Lord, as the apostles did, and we require no more to induce us to submit to him.

But after the Lord had ascended to heaven, the personal call, except in case of Paul, who was one born out of due time, was not the passport of any man either to the ministry or apostleship. Men were no more put into office by the living voice of the Lord Jesus. The departure of the Master, and the vacancy left in the list of apostles by the death of Judas, gave opportunity for bringing into operation a new principle. The first chapter of the Acts of the Apostles brings the whole case before us. Let us specially examine the passage—Acts i. 13–26—that we may have full possession of the facts. It appears that in the interval between the ascension and the day of Pentecost the disciples met for prayer and supplication in an upper room of the city of Jerusalem. The mother and brethren of Jesus were present, as were also the eleven apostles. Taken together, they numbered one hundred and twenty in all. Peter rose and addressed the company. He reminded them of the vacancy in the apostleship. Judas, who betrayed the Master, was dead, and the office that he forfeited by his transgression must be conferred upon another. He states the necessary qualifications of him who was to be the successor of Judas: he must be one who had intercourse with the eleven from the commencement of Christ's ministry to the close. He states the duty of the new apostle: he was to be with the others a witness of Christ's resurrection. Such was the case that Peter put before the men and brethren met together in that upper room of Jerusalem. We then read in verse 23: "THEY AP-POINTED TWO, Joseph called Barsabas, who was surnamed Justus, and Matthias." In consequence of this double choice, it became necessary to decide which should be regarded as the true apostle, which, after prayer, was done by casting lots. But let it be particularly observed that, while Peter explained the necessary qualifications and the peculiar duties of the office, the appointment of the person did not rest with Peter, but with the men and brethren to whom the address of Peter was directed. Further, it is not to be forgotten that the office to which Matthias succeeded is in the 20th verse termed a *bishopric*, and how it is said in the 25th verse, he had "to take part of this *ministry* and apostleship." The men and brethren, at the instigation of Peter, exercised the right of appointing a man to the bishopric—that is, to the office of the bishop—and to take part in the ministry. In the apostolic Church the people appointed Matthias to be a minister— a bishop—an apostle.* The case recorded in

* The argument in reference to the permanent officers of the church will not be weakened if we admit that in setting apart Matthias as an apostle there was no balloting or choice by the church, but that in this case, as well as in that of the other apostles, the Head of the Church directly chose him. We may concede that Justus and Matthias were the only disciples who possessed the necessary qualifications for the apostleship; that "the part performed by the apostles or disciples in this grave transaction was entirely ministerial, and consisted in ascertaining who were eligible, on the principles laid down by Peter, and then placing the man thus selected in the presence of the multitude, or rather before God, as objects of his sovereign choice;" and that the "lots" were not votes or ballots cast by the members of the church, but "the lots of the two candidates"—*i. e.*, the lots which were to choose between them, and were probably

Acts xiv. 23 is to the same effect, though, from a mistranslation, the force of it is lost upon the English reader. The authorized version represents the two apostles, Barnabas and Paul, as *ordaining* elders in every church; whereas the true meaning of the word in the original is "to elect by a show of hands"— a fact now admitted by the best expositors.* We must not allow a faulty translation to rob us of the testimony of Scripture to an important fact—namely, that the elders of the New

inscribed with their respective names," one of which was drawn under the divine guidance, thus showing that Matthias, whose "lot" that was, was the choice of God. We may grant this in reference to the appointment of an apostle who must have companied with the eleven all the time that the Lord Jesus went in and out among them, beginning from the baptism of John unto that same day that he was taken up from them, so that he could with them be a direct witness of the Lord's resurrection, and who, therefore, can have no official successors now living on the earth—we may grant this without weakening the argument, drawn from the other facts quoted in this section, in reference to the election of elders and deacons, the two permanent orders in the Church. P.

* See Dean Alford on the passage.

Testament Church were appointed to office by the popular vote.

The sixth chapter of Acts comes next under consideration. At the period to which the narrative there recorded refers the disciples at Jerusalem had grown numerous. The Grecians began to complain against the Hebrews, how that their widows were neglected in the daily ministrations. Hitherto the twelve had attended to the wants of the poor, but their hands were at the same time full of other work, and among such a multitude, it is not surprising that some were neglected, nor is it very wonderful, considering what human nature is, that some were found to murmur, even when apostles managed the business. What was now to be done? A division of offices was clearly a necessity. But were the apostles to take it on themselves to select persons on whom should devolve the duty of attending to the temporal wants of the community? Had they done so, few would dispute their right, or venture to charge inspired men with the exercise of a despotic or unwarranted authority. But instead of this they adopted a course of procedure unaccountable to us on any other principle than that they purposely managed the matter in such a way as would guide the church in the appointment of officebearers when themselves would be removed, and thus form a precedent for future ages. The apostles summoned the multitude together and explained the case. They said their appropriate business as ministers was with the word of God. They said it was unreasonable for them to have to neglect the spiritual province in order to attend to temporal concerns, and they called upon the brethren to look out from among themselves seven men of good character, gifted with wisdom and the Spirit of God, who might be appointed to take charge of this secular business, and who would leave the apostles free to attend to duties peculiarly their own—namely, prayer and the ministry of the word. "And the saying pleased the whole multitude: and THEY CHOSE Stephen, a man full of faith and of the Holy Ghost, and Philip, and Prochorus, and Nicanor, and Simon, and Parmenas, and Nicolas, a proselyte of Antioch, whom they set before the apostles; and when they had prayed they laid their hands on them." Acts vi. 5, 6. The seven men whom the multitude chose on this occasion were the first *deacons*. Though not expressly called so in the Scriptures, yet they are admitted to have been such by almost universal consent. The lowest office-bearers, therefore, in the apostolic Church, were chosen by the people.

Here, then, are three clear facts fully sufficient to be the basis of a principle. The first chapter of Acts supplies us with an instance of the assembled men and brethren appointing to office one who was both an apostle and a minister. The fourteenth chapter shows that the elders of the congregation were chosen by popular suffrage. The sixth chapter furnishes an example of the whole multitude of the disciples choosing seven men to be deacons. On these three facts, clear and irresistible, we found the principle of POPULAR ELECTION. The conclusion that follows from this evidence we find it absolutely impossible to evade—namely, that in the apostolic Church the *office-bearers were chosen by the people.*

THE SECOND PRINCIPLE.

There is a class of office-bearers very frequently mentioned as existing in the early Church, and to which, as yet, we have only made a slight allusion. We mean the *elder*, or *presbyter*, as he is frequently called. This church-officer is often mentioned in the Acts and Epistles, but an attentive reader will not fail to remark that no passage of Scripture ever speaks of him as holding an office distinct from the *bishop*. The same verse never speaks of bishops and elders. When Paul, for example, writes to the Philippian church (i. 1), he mentions the bishops and deacons, but says nothing of elders. When James directs the sick to call for the elders of the church (v. 14), he says nothing of bishops. If the offices of bishop and elder were quite distinct —if a bishop were an office-bearer bearing rule over a number of elders—it does seem strange that no passage of Scripture speaks at the same time of bishops and elders. There is one supposition, and only one, that would furnish a satisfactory reason for this fact. If the two terms be only different names for the same office, then to speak of *bishops and elders* would be a violation of the laws of language—it would be tautology—it would be the same thing as to speak of presbyters and elders, or of bishops *and* bishops. To suppose that the two offices were identical accounts sufficiently for the significant fact that they are never mentioned together in the same passage of the word of God, for it is plain that, one of the terms being adequate to indicate the office-bearers intended, there was no need to introduce the other at the same time.

Still there must be something stronger than a presumption to warrant us in saying that the two terms were only different names for the same person. However improbable it may appear, it is still possible that these two, bishop and elder, were distinct office-bearers, even though the same passage never speaks of them together. This obliges us to consult the Scriptures further on this question.

The first passage that comes before us is Titus i. 5–7: "For this cause I left thee in Crete, that thou shouldest set in order the things that are wanting, and ordain elders in every city, as I had appointed thee: if any be blameless, the husband of one wife, having faithful children, not accused of riot or unruly. For a bishop must be blameless, as the steward of God; not self-willed, not soon angry, not given to wine, no striker, not given to filthy lucre." This passage strongly confirms the truth of the supposition already made, that the two offices were identical. It appears that Paul left Titus behind him in Crete to ordain elders in every city. To guide him in the discharge of his duty, the apostle proceeds to state the qualifications of an elder. No private member of the church was eligible to that office unless he was a man of blameless life, the husband of one wife, and had obedient children; "for," says he, "a bishop must be blameless, as the steward of God." Dr. King well observes on this passage "that the term *elder*, used at the commencement, is exchanged for the term *bishop* in the conclusion, while the same office-bearer is spoken of. An *elder* must have such and such qualifications. Why? Because a *bishop* must be blameless, as the steward of God. Does not this identify the elder and the bishop? If not, identification is impossible. Were it said the lord mayor of London must devote himself to his duties, for the chief magistrate of such a city has great responsibilities, would not the language indicate that the lord mayor and the chief magistrate were the same office-bearer? Otherwise, the representation would be absurd; for why should the mayor devote himself to his duties because some other person had great responsibilities? Yet the mayor and chief magistrate are not more indentified in this comparison than are the elder and bishop in Paul's instructions to Titus."* It must be evident to every unprejudiced man that the apostle would never state as a reason for ordaining none but men of good moral character to the office of the *eldership*, that a *bishop* must be blameless, if he did not understand

* Dr. King's Exposition and Defence, pp. 176–7. Edinr., 1853.

APOSTOLIC PRINCIPLES. 59

that elder and bishop were only different designations for the same office. On any other supposition the language of the apostle would be without coherence and without sense.

Again, we turn to 2 John i., and we find that the apostle John styles himself an *elder:** "The elder unto the elect lady and her children, whom I love in the truth." Next comes up 1 Peter v. 1, and we find there that the apostle Peter calls himself an *elder:* "The elders which are among you I exhort, who am also an elder, and a witness of the sufferings of Christ." That John and Peter were both bishops all admit, but these passages show that they were elders also. This, however, brings us but a step to the conclusion. It may be true that every general is an officer, but it does not follow from this that every officer is a general. A bishop may, like John and Peter, be an elder, but it does not necessarily follow that an elder is a bishop. This may be true, but we require more proof before we can reach such a conclusion. This we have

* *Presbuteros,* presbyter, elder.

as fully as can be desired in Acts xx. 17–28. We read there how Paul sent for the elders of the church at Ephesus to meet him at Miletus. He spoke of his ministry in their city, the great theme of his preaching being repentance toward God and faith toward the Lord Jesus Christ. He foretold the afflictions awaiting him at Jerusalem and elsewhere, and he saddened their hearts by saying to them that they should see his face no more. And he warned them to take heed to themselves and to "the flock over which the Holy Ghost had made them *overseers*"—that is, *bishops*, as the word is elsewhere rendered. Every reader acquainted with the original is aware that the word translated *overseers*, in Acts xx. 28, is the very same as that translated *bishops* in Phil. i. 1, so that we have here the evidence of inspiration that the elders of Ephesus were bishops by appointment of the Holy Ghost. This makes the chain of reasoning strong and conclusive. Bishops, as we have seen, were elders, and elders, as we now see, were bishops. This conducts us to a second principle—namely, that in THE APOSTOLIC CHURCH

THE OFFICES OF BISHOP AND ELDER WERE IDENTICAL. An elder was not inferior to a bishop, nor was a bishop superior to an elder. It was the same office-bearer who was known by these different names.

We are not disposed to attach much value to the opinion of such a man as Edward Gibbon on any question of doctrine or morality, but that distinguished historian was competent to grapple with a matter of fact, and may be heard as one who, from being unprejudiced in favor of any religious system whatever, was in a position to judge impartially in a case of this kind. Speaking of the government and administration of the Church prior to the Council of Nice, he says, "The public functions of religion were solely entrusted to the established ministers of the Church, bishops and the presbyters, *two appellations which, in their first origin, appear to have distinguished the same office and the same order of persons.* The name of *presbyter* was expressive of their age, or rather of their gravity and wisdom. The title of *bishop* denoted their inspection over the faith and manners of the Christians who were committed to their pastoral care."*

THE THIRD PRINCIPLE.

Let it not be forgotten that we have now ascertained that presbyter and bishop were, in *their origin*, only different names for the same ecclesiastical office-bearer. Enough has been found in the Scriptures to satisfy us that bishops were elders, and that elders were bishops, in the apostolic Church. We are warranted, therefore, to regard this fact as fully substantiated, while we proceed to the discovery of a third principle.

The fourteenth chapter of Acts describes a missionary journey of Paul and Barnabas. There was an attempt made to stone them at Iconium, but they fled to Lystra and Derbe. When Paul made a cripple at Lycaonia leap and walk, the priest of Jupiter brought oxen and garlands to the gates, and it was with some difficulty that the people, in their pagan

* History of the Decline and Fall, chap. xv.

ignorance, were restrained from paying divine honors to the two preachers. But so fickle were the sentiments of the multitude that shortly afterward the great apostle was stoned nearly to death at the very place where he had almost been worshiped as a god. Barely escaping with his life, Paul and his companion revisited Derbe and Lystra, and Iconium and Antioch, preaching the gospel, confirming the souls of the disciples and exhorting them to continue in the faith. And the sacred historian, in the narrative of this evangelistic tour, informs us of this important fact, that *they appointed elders in every church.* His words are: "And when they had chosen for them by suffrage elders in every church, and had prayed with fasting, they commended them to the Lord, on whom they believed." Acts xiv. 23. We have seen already that a Church in Scripture signifies any assembly of Christians, however great or small. It was the primitive practice to call the believers residing in any town, however large, or in any village, however small, the church of that place. Many of these societies, collected from among the heathen by these pioneers of Christianity, organized in the face of difficulty, and thinned by intimidation, must have been weak in point of numbers. Still, the two apostles were not satisfied with appointing one elder or bishop in each society, however small in numbers; but as we are taught by the Holy Spirit, they appointed ELDERS IN EVERY CHURCH. If, then, the evangelist Luke, speaking as he was moved by the Holy Ghost, is a true witness, there were more elders than one in each congregation of the apostolic Church. How many, whether two, three or more, we are not informed, but that in each church there was a plurality of elders is clear.

We proceed once more to the twentieth chapter of Acts. Here Paul is represented as traveling from Greece on his way to Jerusalem. Having stopped a week at Troas, he went upon his onward way, sometimes by sea and sometimes by land, striving to reach the Jewish capital before Pentecost. Having touched at Miletus, a seaport of Ionia, thirty-six miles south of Ephesus, he sent a message to that city for the elders of the Church. The words of inspiration are: "And from Miletus he sent to Ephesus, and called the elders of the Church." Acts xx. 17. From this it appears the church of Ephesus had not only one elder, but more, and we have already seen that in verse 28 its elders are called bishops. Unless language mean nothing, and the statements of Scripture be as unintelligible as the leaves of the Sibyl, there was *a plurality of elders or bishops* in the church at Ephesus.

Still further. Philippi was a city on the confines of ancient Thrace. To the classic reader it is known as the place where Augustus and Anthony wrested from Brutus and Cassius, in a pitched battle, the empire of the world; to the Christian it is remarkable as being the first spot in Europe where the banner of the Cross was unfurled and sinners listened to the gospel of Jesus. There the heart of the seller of purple was opened to attend to the things that were spoken of Paul. It was there that, for casting the spirit of divination out of a soothsayer, Paul and Silas were beaten by the magistrates and had their feet made fast in the stocks. It was there, at the dead hour of night, when the foundations of the prison shook, and every door in the jail flew open, and every man's chains fell from his arms, that the keeper of the prison asked two of his prisoners the most important question that was ever put by a sinner to a minister of God: "Sirs, what must I do to be saved?" In this town of Philippi a church was organized, though in the face of determined opposition, and some ten or twelve years after Paul's first visit he thought it right to address to this church a letter. This letter has been preserved. It finds a place in the word of God. It is that known to us as the Epistle to the Philippians. One has some curiosity to read what an apostle thought it good to write to a church at the head of whose roll of members stood the names of Lydia and the jailer. As might be expected, it is full to the brim of precious and consoling truths; but, what is more to our purpose at present, we find these words in the first verse of the first chapter: "Paul and Timotheus, the servants of Jesus Christ, to all the saints in Jesus Christ which are at Philippi, with THE BISHOPS and deacons." Philippi was, no doubt, a considerable town, but, in point of population and importance, it was no more to such a city as Dublin or Liverpool than a parish is to a diocese. Yet in modern times one bishop is thought sufficient even for London, where professing Christians are numbered by millions, whereas a single Christian congregation gathered out of a heathen population, possessing ecclesiastical existence only for ten or twelve years, exposed to contumely and suffering for Christ's sake, and located in a contemptible town on the outskirts of Macedonia, had a *plurality of bishops*. Paul, in writing to that Church, addresses his Epistle to the *bishops* and deacons.

Let the candid reader glance again at the ground over which we have passed. He sees that Paul, in writing his Epistle to the church at Philippi, addressed it to the *bishops*. He sees there were *elders* in the church at Ephesus when Paul sent for them to Miletus. He finds it stated that Barnabas and Paul ordained *elders in every church*. How is it possible for him to resist the conclusion that in apostolic days there was in each congregation a plurality of elders, or, what we have seen amounts to the same thing, a plurality of bishops? This leads us to the third principle of apostolic government—that IN EACH CHURCH THERE WAS A PLURALITY OF ELDERS.

THE FOURTH PRINCIPLE.

Ordination is the solemn designation of a person to ecclesiastical office with the laying on of hands. Every permanent office-bearer in the Church, whether bishop or deacon, was set apart solemnly to his office by the act of ordination. In its outward form it consisted of three things—fasting, prayer and imposition of hands. The imposition of hands was used when spiritual gifts were conferred (Acts viii. 17; xix. 6), and it was also practiced when the sick were miraculously healed. Mark xxvi. 18; Acts ix. 17; xxviii. 8. But, distinct from all such cases, the laying on of hands was used at the ordination of Church

APOSTOLIC PRINCIPLES.   69

office-bearers, and when no extraordinary or miraculous gift was bestowed. Acts vi. 6; xiii. 1-3; and 1 Tim. iv. 14; v. 22. The withdrawment of miraculous powers cannot therefore be any valid reason why, at ordinations, the practice should be set aside; the imposition of hands in such cases never was the medium of imparting the Holy Ghost, but only the form of investing with ecclesiastical office.

The great question regarding ordination is whether it is the act of one individual or more, of one elder or many elders, of a bishop or a presbytery. That the Lord Jesus may give a special call to any laborer, and send him to work in his vineyard, none disputes. There can be very little doubt also that if an inspired apostle were still upon the earth, he would have the right to ordain alone, if he thought it right to do so. Nay, if some modern evangelist could show, as Titus could, that an apostle had left him behind for this special purpose, he, too, in virtue of the right conferred upon him by a higher power, would have the privilege of ordaining. Titus i. 5.

Any one, therefore, claiming the right of doing all that an evangelist did, would require to show that, if not an apostle, he possesses, like Titus, the authority delegated to him by an apostle. But here every ruler in every Church must fail. It remains, therefore, that we examine the Scriptures to discover who it was that in the absence of apostles, or those delegated by apostles, had the privilege of solemnly setting apart others to ecclesiastical office, and especially to ascertain if this power was lodged in one individual or in more.

First, we turn to 1 Tim. iv. 14. We have there the ordination of Timothy. The apostle exhorts his son in the faith to employ to good purpose the gift of the ministry that had been conferred upon him. He intimates that this gift had been given by prophecy—that is, in consequence of certain intimations of the prophets, who were numerous in that age of spiritual gifts, marking him out as one who would be an eminent minister. He adds that the gift was conferred *with the laying on of the hands of the presbytery*—that is, by the presbyters or elders in their collective capacity.

The words of the apostle are: "Neglect not the gift that is in thee, which was given thee by prophecy, WITH THE LAYING ON OF THE HANDS OF THE PRESBYTERY." These words are decisive as to the parties with whom the power of ordination is lodged.

Again, we turn to Acts xiii. 1–3. It appears that in the church of Antioch there were certain prophets and teachers whose names are there recorded. They ministered to the Lord and fasted; and while thus employed, it was intimated to them by the Holy Ghost that they should separate Barnabas and Saul for missionary work among the Gentiles. Both had been preachers of the gospel previously, but now they were to enter on a new sphere, and engage in a new department of the work. It was right, therefore, that the prophets and teachers should solemnly set apart the two brethren to the missionary work by the act of ordination. We read, accordingly, in verse 3, that "when *they* had fasted and prayed, and *laid their hands on them*, they sent them away." The act of ordination was here evidently not the work of one teacher, but of several. A plurality took part in it.

Another instance of plurality of Church rulers taking part in this rite is recorded in Acts vi. 6. We have there the ordination of the deacons. The church at Jerusalem chose seven men to attend to the necessities of the poor, "whom they set before the apostles: and when they had prayed, *they laid their hands upon them.*" This is particularly valuable, as it proves that when it was convenient or practicable for a plurality of rulers to take part in the act of ordination, the apostles themselves preferred that course.

Glance again at the ground over which we have now passed. It was the practice of an apostle, or one directly appointed by an apostle for this specific purpose, to perform alone the act of ordination. But they did not ordain singly where it was possible for them to associate. Where a plurality could be had conveniently, as in the case of the deacons, it was common for more than one to take part in the ceremony. In the absence of apostles we have seen, in the case of Saul and Barnabas, ordination was the act of certain prophets and teachers, and in the case of Timothy it was the act of the presbytery. This conducts us to our fourth principle—namely, that IN THE APOSTOLIC CHURCH ORDINATION WAS THE ACT OF THE PRESBYTERY, of a plurality of elders.

THE FIFTH PRINCIPLE.

The fifteenth chapter of Acts is much too long to be here transcribed, but before the reader proceeds farther let him open the Bible and read that chapter carefully from the commencement to the close. If he is really in search of truth, and disposed to receive it in its simplicity, the perusal of that chapter will satisfy him that the following facts are there embodied:

It appears that certain men came down from Judea to Antioch, and taught the church there that circumcision is necessary to salvation. Paul and Barnabas set themselves to oppose these teachers, but in vain. It was then agreed that certain of the church of

Antioch, including in their number Barnabas and Paul, should go up to Jerusalem and lay the case before the apostles and elders. When they reached Jerusalem—at that time the metropolis of Christianity—the apostles and elders came together to consider the question. At first there was in the assembly considerable difference of opinion. Peter at last rose to speak. He reminded them how God had honored him in making him the instrument of first preaching the gospel to the Gentiles, and how it had pleased God, without respect of persons, to bestow the Holy Ghost upon them as well as upon Jewish believers. He argues, therefore, that to make circumcision necessary to salvation—to bind a yoke upon the Gentiles which even the Jews were not able to bear—would be to tempt God; and he closes by enunciating the great truth that Jews and Gentiles, both alike, obtain salvation through the grace of our Lord Jesus Christ. Barnabas and Paul followed, declaring that by them, too, God had wrought among the Gentiles miracles and wonders. James next delivered his opinion. He showed that the truth declared by Peter—namely, that God had taken out of the Gentiles a people for his name—was the subject of ancient prophecy. He quotes from the prophet Amos to show how God had promised to build the tabernacle of David, which had fallen into ruins, that the residue of men and the Gentiles called by his name should seek after the Lord. He ends by declaring his judgment to be that the Gentiles already turned to the Lord should not be troubled with any unnecessary burden, but that they should be directed to abstain from pollutions of idols, and from fornication, and from things strangled, and from blood.

The opinion of James was approved by the assembly. The apostles and elders, with the whole Church, agreed to send Judas and Silas down to Antioch, with Barnabas and Paul, to announce the result. The decision of the meeting was embodied in letters which ran in the name of the apostles, elders and brethren, and were addressed to the Gentile Christians in Antioch, Syria and Cilicia.

The epistle charged those who taught that

circumcision was necessary to salvation with troubling the brethren and subverting their souls; denied that they had authority from the apostles and elders so to teach; mentioned that Judas and Silas were empowered, along with Barnabas and Paul—men who hazarded their lives for the name of the Lord Jesus—to declare verbally the decision of the assembly; and stated that it seemed good to the Holy Ghost and to them to impose upon the Gentile converts no burden except abstinence from meats offered to idols, from blood, from things strangled and from fornication.

Such was the substance of the letter that was carried down to Antioch by the deputies from the assembly at Jerusalem. The multitude gathered to hear it; it was delivered and read, and the people rejoiced for the consolation. Judas and Silas added their exhortations, and the brethren were confirmed in the faith.

Shortly afterward, Paul, having had some difference with Barnabas, chose Silas as his fellow-traveler, and set out on another missionary journey, the object of which was to visit the converts in every city where he had preached the word of God, and see how they did. Commended by the brethren to the grace of God, Paul and Silas departed from Antioch, and went through Syria and Cilicia confirming the churches. Derbe and Lystra and other cities of Asia Minor were visited on this occasion; and as they went through the cities, they delivered to them the decrees for to keep which were ordained of the apostles and elders that were at Jerusalem. Acts xvi. 4.

Every candid man must admit that this is a fair representation of all the facts bearing on the subject, as put before us in the fifteenth and sixteenth chapters of the Acts. Let it be remarked that in the simple narrative the following facts stand noticeably out: 1. That Barnabas and Paul had a dispute about circumcision with certain false teachers who came down from Judea. 2. This dispute was not settled in the church of Antioch, where it originated. 3. The matter was referred to an external ecclesiastical assembly consisting of the apostles and elders at Jerusalem. 4. This assembly met publicly to deliberate on the question. 5. They pronounced a decision. 6. To this decision the church of Antioch and the churches of Syria and Cilicia yielded submission.

These facts are on the face of the narrative, and cannot be denied. That they were permitted to take place, and that a record of them is inserted in the Holy Scriptures, seems strange if these things did not happen for an example to us. Were it enough for the church of Antioch to be made certain of the mind of God upon the point in dispute, Paul, who was present, could have declared this with infallible accuracy, for he was one who not only spake as he was moved by the Holy Ghost, but who often decided matters equally important by a word from his lips or a stroke of his pen. A single sentence from the very apostle who was then at Antioch is admitted by the Church of God to be decisive on any point of Christian faith or Christian duty; so that if an infallible decision was the only thing required, one does not see why the matter was ever carried farther. When the case

APOSTOLIC PRINCIPLES. 79

did come up to Jerusalem, had the appeal been to inspiration only, one does not see what business the elders had to meet with the apostles to consider the matter; surely the apostles were competent to declare the mind of God without the aid of uninspired men. If nothing was necessary but for the apostles to pronounce an infallible deliverance, why was there such a thing as disputing in the assembly, or even the semblance of deliberation, or why should one apostle after another state his opinion? We would suppose the deliverance of a single inspired man quite sufficient. If the disputing that occurred in the assembly was only among the elders, the elders must have been very silly to dispute about a matter that inspiration was to settle, and with which they, as uninspired men, could have nothing to do but to listen to the voice of God; and why did the apostles permit them to dispute, when a word from the infallible expounders of the divine will could have decided the question? And when the decree went forth, why was it in the name of the apostles and *elders* that were at Jerusalem? There is one way of accounting for this satisfactorily, and only one, so far as we can see. These events were permitted to take place and are recorded for our guidance under all similar circumstances. Should any difference arise which cannot be settled within the limits of the congregation where it occurs, it is to be referred for settlement to the rulers of the church in their assembled capacity. If the apostles were alive upon the earth to meet with the elders, and by aid of their inspiration to guide them to an unerring decision, and were we to refer our differences to such an assembly, this would be literal obedience to the example put before us in the divine word. But when, in their personal absence, we refer our differences to the assembly of the elders, and when the elders, guided by the inspired writings of the apostles as contained in the Scriptures, pronounce a deliverance on the question, and when to such deliverance we yield submission in the Lord, this is more than acting up to the spirit, it is acting up to everything but the letter, of apostolic example.

We are thus conducted to the twofold fact

that in the apostolic Church there existed the privilege of referring disputed matters to the decision of an assembly of living men external to the congregation where such dispute originated, and composed of the rulers of the church; and that this ecclesiastical assembly, in the absence of the apostles consisting simply of the rulers of the church, has a right to meet, to deliberate, to decide and to demand obedience to its decisions in the Lord. This twofold principle we designate *the privilege of appeal to the assembly of elders, and the right of government exercised by them in their associate capacity.*

It would scarcely be necessary to say a word on the presence of the *brethren* in the assembly at Jerusalem, were it not that some parties have made this fact the foundation for special cavil. As they are mentioned separately from the apostles and elders, it seems to us clear that the "brethren" must have been the non-official members of the church, or, as in modern times they would be called, the laity. That they were present at the meeting, that they concurred in the decision and that the letter sent down to Antioch was written in their name, as well as in that of the apostles and elders, are, in our opinion, undeniable facts—patent on the face of the narrative. But we have not all the facts of the case before us, except we observe, *first*, that the original reference from Antioch was not to the brethren, but to the apostles and elders (verse 2); *second*, that it is not said that the brethren assembled to deliberate on the question, but that "the apostles and elders came together for to consider of this matter" (verse 6); *third*, that we do not read of any of the brethren speaking on the subject submitted, but that they "kept silence" while others spoke (verse 12); *fourth*, that the decrees are not said to be ordained of the brethren, but "of the apostles and elders which were at Jerusalem." Acts xvi. 4. The unprejudiced inquirer will observe that the private members of the church, here designated the "brethren," did not ordain the decrees, nor speak in the meeting, nor assemble to deliberate, nor was it to them that the appeal from Antioch was brought. He will, on the other hand, remark that they were present in the assembly, that they concurred in the finding, and that, as it was important to show that all the Christians of Jerusalem were unanimous on the subject, the letter embodying the decision was written in their name as well as in that of the apostles and elders. From motives of courtesy, and for 'the purpose of Christian salutation, Silvanus and Timotheus are represented as uniting with Paul in his First Epistle to the Thessalonians, but this does not imply that Silvanus and Timotheus were inspired men, much less that they were conjoined in the authorship of the letter. And, in the same way, the letter addressed to the Gentiles of Antioch, Syria and Cilicia was the letter of the apostles and elders, the name of the brethren being added to show, not that they took part in the composition, but that they concurred in the sentiments. Persons, therefore, who desire to convince us that private Christians in the apostolic Church were not only present as auditors at assemblies of church rulers, but also shared in the deliberations, and acted as constituent members of ecclesiastical courts, would require to produce something much more explicit on the subject than the 15th chapter of Acts. To us it seems clear that the apostles and elders assembled, deliberated and decreed; the brethren were present, listened and concurred. The apostles and elders were, as we would say, members of court; the brethren were only auditors who gave their assent to the decision of the rulers.

Our fifth principle, therefore, may be summed up in these terms: THE PRIVILEGE OF APPEAL TO THE ASSEMBLY OF ELDERS, AND THE RIGHT OF GOVERNMENT EXERCISED BY THEM IN THEIR CORPORATE CHARACTER.

THE SIXTH PRINCIPLE.

It is a distinctive feature of the apostolic government that church rulers did not render spiritual obedience to any temporal potentate or to any ecclesiastical chief. Paul seldom commences any of his Epistles without reminding his readers that he held his apostleship by the will of God, not by the favor of man. Take, as an example, Gal. i. 1: "Paul an apostle (not of men, neither by man, but by Jesus Christ, and God the Father who raised him from the dead)," etc. In the picture of apostolic times presented in the New Testament, we can detect no instance of the Church acknowledging the spiritual dominion of any earthly monarch, or consenting to surrender a portion of its religious liberty for any temporal advantage whatever. We find no provision made in the gospel for the supremacy of a Christian, much less of a heathen, king in the things of God. The law of Scripture is express: "Render to Cæsar the things that are Cæsar's, and to God the things that are God's." Mark xii. 17. In all temporal matters the members of the apostolic Church regarded it their duty to yield obedience to the civil rulers of the country in which they lived; in all spiritual matters they did homage to a higher power. In temporal matters an apostle bowed to the laws of the land as administered by the magistrate of a village; in spiritual matters he would not bow to Cæsar on his throne.

It does not alter the case to say that we look in vain for such an example in the Scriptures, owing to the fact that in the primitive age no temporal prince was made a convert to Christianity, and therefore none was in circumstances to dispense ecclesiastical patronage and serve as the depositary of spiritual power. But God is not limited by want of instruments. The same grace that subdued Saul of Tarsus, at a time when he was breathing out slaughter against the saints of the Lord, could have converted Pilate, or Agrippa, or Cæsar at Rome. Had the example been useful, the necessary means of supplying the example would not have been lacking to God. The very fact that in apostolic days God did not take some heathen prince and make a Christian of him, in order that he might fill the office of temporal head of the Church on earth, is in itself an instructive fact, fraught with a moral. And let it be remarked that the Scriptures make no provision for such an occurrence in after times.

APOSTOLIC PRINCIPLES. 87

They contain no principle authorizing the prince either to claim or exercise authority in ecclesiastical matters, when, in the course of ages, a Christian potentate would appear. If there be such a principle, it is unknown to us; and it is certainly incumbent on those who approve of such an arrangement, to produce from the Scriptures, if they can, their warrant for maintaining that a Christian king has a right to exercise supremacy over the Church in spiritual matters. Till this is done we must be excused for believing that no temporal prince has a right to act as a lord over the heritage of God.

Nor was supreme spiritual power lodged in the hands of any office-bearer of the church, however distinguished by his gifts, his sufferings or his abundant labors. The private members, indeed, had it in command to obey the rulers or elders of the church, but the elders, on their part, were enjoined not to act as lords over God's heritage, but to be examples to the flock. 1 Pet. v. 3. Even the apostles did not claim to have dominion over the people's faith, but only to be helpers of their joy. 2 Cor. i. 24. And among these apostles it does not appear that pre-eminence was vested in any. Peter is the only one for whom, in later times, official supremacy is ever claimed, but he never claimed it for himself; he always acted with his fellow-apostles as a simple preacher of the cross of Christ; he is never presented in the Scriptures as nominating to ecclesiastical office, or as exercising any peculiar control over the inferior officers in the church. On one noted occasion, when he exhibited some tergiversation, we are told of another apostle who withstood him to the face, because he was to be blamed. Gal. ii. 11. The Scripture, therefore, furnishes no ground whatever for believing that supreme spiritual power is deposited in any ecclesiastical officer any more than in any temporal prince.

The Scriptures are to be our guide on this as well as all other religious matters. We turn to the following passages, and find where the source of all spiritual power exists:

Eph. i. 20-23: "Which he [God] wrought in Christ, when he raised him from the dead, and set him at his own right hand in the heavenly places, far above all principality and power, and might and dominion, and every name that is named, not only in this world, but also in that which is to come, and hath put all things under his feet, and gave *him to be head over all things to the Church*, which is his body, the fullness of him that filleth all in all."

Eph. v. 23: "For the husband is the head of the wife, even *as Christ is the head of the Church;* and he is the Saviour of the body."

Col. i. 18: "And he [Christ] *is the head of the body, the Church;* who is the beginning, the first-born from the dead; that in all things he might have the pre-eminence."

The passages now quoted are taken from the Holy Scriptures—the only rule of Christian faith and practice. We have given them our attentive consideration, and they have led us to the conclusion that *the sole headship of Christ over the Church* was the doctrine of apostolic days. What the head is to the human body Christ is to the Church; and as the body cannot have two heads, so the Church cannot have two heads—neither Christ and the pope, nor Christ and the monarch. To us there seems no middle way in this matter. We must either reject the authority of the Bible, or believe what it teaches—namely, that *Christ is head over all things to the Church.* We choose the latter. The HEADSHIP OF CHRIST is the sixth principle of government that we find in operation in apostolic days. Let us observe the consequence of this principle; for, as Christ is the head of the Church, the members of the Church are to be subject to him; and, as we have no other way of ascertaining the mind of Christ except through the Scriptures, it follows that the affairs of the Church are to be managed by those officers whom the Lord Jesus has entrusted with that power, and are, without the interference of any external authority, to be regulated according to the mind of God as expressed in his word.

APPLICATION OF THE TEST.

LET the reader seriously consider the evidence submitted in the previous chapter, and we think he will be satisfied that there is divine authority for saying that the principles of which the following facts are the realization were in practical operation in the apostolic Church:

1. The office-bearers were chosen by the people.

2. The office of bishop was identical with that of elder.

3. There was a plurality of elders in each church.

4. Ordination was the act of a presbytery —that is, of a plurality of elders.

5. There was the privilege of appeal to the assembly of elders; and the power of government was exercised by them in their associate capacity.

6. The only Head of the Church was the Lord Jesus Christ.

The principles embodied in these six facts cover the whole platform of church government, each rising in importance above that which precedes it, in an ascending series, from popular election up to the headship of the Lord. We have been conducted to them, not by any process of wire-drawn logic, but by receiving the Scriptures, as we think every child of God should receive them, except there be manifest and good reasons to the contrary, in the plain, simple and natural sense. The most unlettered reader, if he be only unprejudiced and honest, cannot examine the passages of Scripture we have specified and fail to see that these six great principles were all embodied in the government of the apostolic Church. But whether they are embodied in those forms of ecclesiastical government at present existing in the world is another and a very important question—a question which it is now our business to answer. We proceed, therefore, to bring the existing systems in succession to the test of the apostolic standard.

PRELACY.

As already explained, prelacy is that system of church government which is dispensed by archbishops, bishops, priests, deans, deacons and other office-bearers.* It is exemplified in the Church of Rome and in the Church of England, both of which are prelatic in their government, the difference being that the prelacy of Rome vests the ecclesiastical supremacy in the pope, while the prelacy of England vests it in the reigning monarch. With this exception, the two Churches, however widely they may differ in doctrine, are in every important point of government the same. As many may be disposed to consider the prelacy of the Protestant Church much less objectionable than the prelacy of Rome, and as we have neither necessity nor desire to take any unfair advantage in argument, we prefer to bring the prelacy of Protestantism into comparison with the apostolic standard.

The fountain of jurisdiction in the Church of England is the monarch for the time being, who inherits the throne by hereditary descent,

* See note on page 11.

and who, irrespective of all character, is, by act of Parliament, the only supreme head of the Church of England and Ireland. [37 Henry VIII., chap. 17.] No person can be received into the ministry of that Church till he subscribe this article: "That the king's majesty, under God, is the only supreme governor of this realm, and of all other his highness' dominions and countries, *as well in all spiritual or ecclesiastical things* or causes as temporal." [*Canon* 36.] The appointment of all the archbishops and bishops is vested in the crown, which is guided in the selection by the political administration of the day—a body composed of every hue of religious profession, and only kept in its place by the majority of votes it can command in Parliament. The highest ecclesiastical office-bearers under the crown are the archbishops, of whom there are two in England—the archbishops of Canterbury and York—and two in Ireland—the archbishops of Armagh and Dublin.* Each of these has under him a number of suffragan

---

* Since the publication of this book, the Irish Episcopal Church has been disestablished.   P.

bishops, and each bishop has under his care the inferior clergy of his diocese, who preach and dispense the ordinances of religion to such inhabitants of their parish as are pleased to receive them. The parish clergy are in some instances appointed by the crown, in others by the bishop, in others by a lay patron, and sometimes in a mode still more objectionable.

Such is prelacy as presented in the Protestant Establishment of England. Let us compare it with the system of government which we have already ascertained to exist in the apostolic Church.

In the apostolic Church the office-bearers were chosen by the people, but in the Church of England archbishops are chosen by the crown, and the subordinate clergy are appointed to their charges either by the diocesan or by some landed proprietor, or by some civil corporation. The people of the apostolic Church exercised the privilege of electing an apostle; the people in the Church of England have not power to elect a curate.

In the apostolic Church the office of bishop and elder was identical; the elders of Ephesus were the bishops of the flock; but in the English Church Establishment it is very different. The apostolic elder, being a teacher and ruler of a congregation, resembles more closely the parish clergyman than any other office-bearer in the Church of England. But it is very evident that in that church a parish clergyman holds a position widely different from a bishop. The rector wields the jurisdiction of a parish, but the bishop governs a diocese, that usually includes a whole multitude of parishes. The one presides over a single congregation, the other over many congregations. The one exercises authority over the laity, but a Church of England bishop is the ruler of a band of clergy. If, then, the parish clergyman correspond to the presbyter or elder of apostolic times, it is very clear that in the Establishment the bishop and elder are not identical in office. In the Established Church every elder is subject to his bishop, but in the apostolic Church every elder was a bishop himself.

In the Church of England each congregation is under the care of one presbyter. When a second is called in, he is a mere curate in the employment of another, and void of all ecclesiastical jurisdiction. It is not very common, and certainly not essential to the system, to have more than one presbyter or elder in one church; whereas we have seen that in each church in apostolic times there was a plurality of elders.

In the Church of England ordination is an act exclusively performed by a prelate; he may ask others to unite with him, but it is his presence, not theirs, that is essential to the act; whereas in the apostolic Church it was the practice to ordain men to the office of the ministry with the laying on of the hands of the presbytery.

In the Church of England, no matter what ecclesiastical grievance may exist, there is no power of appeal except to the courts of law, or the queen's privy council, or some such tribunal. The practice is unknown in the denomination of bringing any matter for consideration before the assembly of elders for them to decide upon in accordance with the apostles' word. But this, as we have seen, was the mode in which affairs were managed in the apostolic Church.

In our Protestant Establishment the monarch is, by act of Parliament, head of the Church, and to the king or queen, as the case may be, the 37th Article informs us that "the chief government of all estates of the realm, whether they be ecclesiastical or civil, *in all causes*, doth appertain;" whereas in apostolic times the Church had no head but Jesus Christ.*

We have thus examined and compared the

---

* The Protestant Episcopal Church in the United States exhibits some modifications in the particulars specified in the text. Each congregation chooses its vestrymen and wardens, and these officers elect the rector of the church. The annual and general conventions have a power of legislation in reference to the affairs of the sect at large. It has not yet any archbishops, nor in the dioceses generally deans or archdeacons, though in Illinois, we believe, an attempt has been made to develop these officers. In other respects the statements of the text will apply to the denomination in this country as well as to the English Establishment. Though its allegiance to the head of the Anglican Church has been dissolved, it retains the peculiarities by which that Church is distinguished from all other Protestant denominations, and it looks up to it as its mother Church.   P.

two Churches as closely and candidly as it is possible for us to do, and we feel ourselves forced to the conclusion that, of the six great principles of ecclesiastical government that met in the apostolic Church, there is not one embodied in the prelacy of the Church of England. We infer, therefore, that, while that Church may be entitled to great respect as a human system, maintained by act of Parliament, and numbering in its ranks many estimable people, there is no ground whatever for regarding it, in point of government, as an apostolic Church. At the peril of excommunication, we feel bound to declare our conviction that the government of the Church of England is repugnant to the word of God.*

* No. VII. of the *Constitutions and Canons Ecclesiastical*, agreed upon with the king's license in 1603, and republished by the Prayer-Book and Homily Society (1852), is as follows: "Whosoever shall hereafter affirm that the government of the Church of England under his Majesty by archbishops, bishops, deans, archdeacons and the rest that bear office in the same is anti-Christian or repugnant to the word of God, let him be excommunicated *ipso facto*, and so continue till he repent and publicly revoke such his wicked errors."

INDEPENDENCY AND CONGREGATIONALISM.

It is difficult to ascertain the particulars of ecclesiastical order approved by Independents, inasmuch as we are not aware that they have embodied their views of what the Scriptures teach on the subject in any common formula, and as every congregation, standing apart from every other, may differ sometimes widely on important points. We are, therefore, left to discover their views of church polity from the general practices known to exist among them, and from the principles advocated by their most eminent writers. These, however, are sufficiently known to enable us to compare the Independent system of church government with the apostolic standard.

The principle of popular election existed, as we have seen, in the primitive Church, and had the sanction of the apostles of the Lord. Among the Independents this principle is preserved in its integrity; with them every ecclesiastical office-bearer is chosen by the people.

In the apostolic Church the office of bishop

and elder was identical; the bishop did not exercise any authority over the elder; on the contrary, every bishop was an elder, and every elder a bishop. So it is with Independents. Every one of their pastors fills the office of bishop and elder, and none of them claims authority over others. With them a bishop and elder are only different names for the same office-bearers, as it was in apostolic days.

We have seen how, in apostolic times, there was a plurality of elders in each church. Here the Independent system fails. On the principles of that theory of church government, it is scarcely possible to have a plurality of elders, and in practice it rarely, if ever, occurs. Among them there is only one minister, or bishop, or elder, in each congregation. Practically, their system admits only of one elder to each church. If an apostle were writing an epistle to an Independent church, he would never think of addressing it to the *bishops*, as well as to the deacons, for the simple reason that with them there is usually but *one* bishop to one church; nor could an apostle ever send for the *elders* of an Independent church, as Paul sent for the elders of Ephesus, for the plain reason that in an Independent church there is usually but one elder. A single pastor, with deacons under him, is the prominent feature that the Independent system everywhere presents—an arrangement than which none can be more opposed to the plurality of elders that existed in each congregation in primitive times. Some Independents attempt to palliate their departure from apostolic precedent by saying that a plurality of elders is desirable, but their churches are not able to support them. Does it never strike our esteemed brethren that there must be some remarkable disparity between the apostolic system and theirs, when the richest of their churches now cannot afford to possess what was possessed by the very poorest churches in the days of the apostles? It is the word of God that says of Paul and Barnabas, "They ordained elders in *every* church."

The office-bearers of the apostolic Church were set apart to the discharge of their peculiar duties with the laying on of the hands of the presbytery. Among Independents, however, ordination of any sort is not essential; frequently it is counted unnecessary. Instances are known of persons acting as pastors of churches for a lifetime, who were never inducted to office with the imposition of hands and prayer. Ordination is not required by the system. With them it is a mere matter of taste, left in each case to the individual choice. If the newly-elected pastor choose to have himself ordained, it can only be done in a way inconsistent with Independent principles. The congregation being destitute of a plurality of elders, his ordination can only come from the people, who have no scriptural right to confer it, or from the neighboring pastors. But who does not see that the latter practice is entirely at variance with the foundation principles of Independency, namely—that each congregation has *within* itself complete materials for government? So much is this felt to be the case that, while some ask the assistance of the pastors of the district on such occasions, those who choose to carry out their

Congregationalist principle with a little more consistency make light of ordination, think it unnecessary and prefer to go without it.*

* The Congregationalism of the United States is founded on these principles. It invests all ecclesiastical power (under Christ) in the membership of each local church as an independent body. It recognizes, however, a fellowship between these independent churches which invests each with the right and duty of *advice*. In that respect it differs from Independency, which ignores any check even of advice upon the action of particular congregations. Ordination is not essential in Congregationalism. It is held that there is no command for its continuance, though it has a pleasant fitness which keeps up the practice of it. When performed, it is nothing but the solemn installation of a functionary, previously appointed, in the place to which he has been chosen—the consummation of the act of election, and it means precisely the same, whether applied to pastor, deacons, clerk, treasurer or committees. Each congregation has in itself the power to ordain, but it is a matter of comity to invite neighboring churches, by their representatives, pastoral and lay, to pronounce the benediction upon the consummation of the *pastoral* union. The pastor of a particular congregation, as well as its deacons, clerk and treasurer, should be selected from its own membership. When a man ceases to be the pastor of a church, he falls back to the position of a private member in it. If he takes his membership to another congregation, and is elected pastor there, he must be again ordained, though all

In the apostolic Church there was the privilege of appeal to the assembly of elders. Among the Independents nothing of this kind can exist. The distinctive principle of their system precludes all appeal. The decision of the pastor and deacons and people, assembled in a church-meeting, is final in every case. No matter how partial or unjust their decision is felt to be, there is no power of bringing the sentence under review of a less prejudiced and more enlightened tribunal. The judgment of the Church may be in strict accordance with justice, or it may be the offspring of prejudice or malevolence in a few of the leaders of the meeting, masked, of course, under zeal for purity of communion and for the cause of religion; but no matter how superficial the investigation or how deep the wrong, the system deprives the injured man

ordinations after the first are usually styled installations. (See Dexter's "Congregationalism;" especially pp. 1, 2, and 136-146.) These statements show that what is said in the text in reference to ordination among English Independents applies substantially to the Congregational theory of this country. The other features of Independency as described above also belong to it. P.

of the privilege of appeal, and clothes the perpetrators with irresponsible power. By denying and repudiating all association, it enables the rulers to be, if they please, the tyrants of the Church, and strips the injured of the possibility of redress. "Independency," says Dr. Wardlaw, "is the *competency* of every distinct Church to manage, *without appeal*, its own affairs."* This is an ingenious mode of disguising the most repulsive feature of the system. Very few would deny that a church is competent to manage its own affairs in such a way as to obviate the necessity of appeal; but what we assert is that when the Church lacks the necessary wisdom and discretion to do so, appeal among Independents is not permitted, the injured is deprived of redress, and power, for which the possessor is irresponsible to man, degenerates into tyranny when it is unwisely exercised, and there is nothing to keep it in check. The case of Antioch shows that when a difference arose in the primitive Church, there was a right of referring the

* Dr. Wardlaw's "Congregational Independency;" p. 232, Glasgow, 1848.

matter to the assembly of elders, who, under the guidance of the apostles, settled the business. Elders might still meet, and the written word of the apostles is accessible to all, and a decision pronounced by parties removed from the scene of controversy, untainted by local prejudices, and standing far away from the partisanship of the leaders, might go far now, as in ancient days, to calm dissensions, should they unfortunately arise. But Independents, in this respect, repudiate the apostolic example. Their principle is to refuse all recognition of external authority, to make the decision of the church-meeting final in every case, and to deny to them who are aggrieved the privilege of appeal.*

* The Baptists are independent or congregational in their form of government. Dr. Wayland, in his "Notes on the Principles and Practices of the Baptist Churches," says (p. 177): "The Baptists have ever believed in the entire and absolute independency of the churches. By this we mean that every church of Christ—that is, every company of believers united together according to the laws of Christ—is perfectly capable of self-government, and that, therefore, no one acknowledges any higher authority under Christ than itself; that with the church all ecclesiastical action commences, and with it termi-

The Headship of Christ was a principle of apostolic times. Independents, we are happy to say, acknowledge this principle in all its integrity.

The result of our comparison is, that there are three principles of the apostolic Church that we find fully acknowledged and acted upon among our Independent brethren — namely, popular election, the identity of presbyter and bishop, and the Headship of Christ over the Church. But there are three apostolic

nates; and hence, that the ecclesiastical relations proper of every member are limited to the church to which he belongs." In striking inconsistency with this, however, as to ordination, which is certainly a very important part of the "self-government" of each Church, Dr. Wayland says (p. 114): "A single church does not ordain. It calls a council, generally representing the churches in the vicinity, who are present by their ministers and such private brethren as they may select." The associations and councils of the Baptists and Congregationalists are practical departures from the fundamental principle of their form of government, and a half-way adoption, for general church work, of some of the features of Presbyterianism. No appeal, however, lies to the associations from individual churches, nor have they, in reference to particular church questions, the right to do anything more than advise. P.

principles that we fail to find in their system—namely, the plurality of elders in each church, ordination with the laying on of the hands of the presbytery, and the privilege of appeal. We conclude, therefore, that, while the Independent system of government advances to the pattern of primitive times much more closely than that which exists in the churches of England and Rome, still, it is not the system entitled to plead the precedent of the apostolic Church.

PRESBYTERY.

It only now remains that we compare the Presbyterian system with the standard of the law and of the testimony. The term *Presbyterian* is derived from the word *presbytery*, because the leading characteristic of this form of church government is, that it entrusts the duty of ruling the Church to the presbytery—that is, to the presbyters or elders of the Church in their assembled capacity. But let us bring it, as well as the others, to the scriptural standard.

In the apostolic Church we have mentioned frequently already that popular election was an admitted principle. It is so with Presbyterians. In all Presbyterian churches throughout Britain and America, with the single exception of the Established Church of Scotland, the members of each congregation invariably elect their own office-bearers. The privilege has been abused sometimes, as what good thing has not been abused by the sin and infatuation of man? But it is a scriptural privilege that the apostolic Church bequeaths us, and Presbyterians have often shown that they count it more precious than gold.

In the primitive age the office of bishop and elder was identical. An elder was not inferior, in point of official standing, to a bishop, nor a bishop to an elder. It is so in the Presbyterian Church. Every elder is a bishop or overseer of the flock, and every bishop is an elder, one whose office is to rule in the house of God. There are two departments in the office of the elder—that of teaching, and that of ruling; but the office itself is one.

There was a plurality of elders or bishops in each congregation of the apostolic Church. Such is the practice in every Presbyterian church at the present day. There is in each of their congregations a number of persons ordained to the office of the eldership, one of whom at least gives himself to the work of the ministry in its various departments, particularly that of public instruction, while the others give their principal attention to ruling in the Church of God. Teaching and ruling, as we have already stated, are different departments of the same office; and while there can be no doubt that those appointed to the office have, in the abstract, a right to fill both departments, yet, in practice, it is found more convenient and beneficial for the people that each elder give most of his attention to that department whose duties he is best qualified to discharge. All elders, being bishops, would have an equal right, according to the Scriptures, to preach, baptize, administer the Lord's Supper and ordain; but these duties it is arranged to devolve on one of the elders, called by distinction the *minister*, who is especially trained to his work, and is, by general consent, admitted to possess most gifts and attainments, and who, in consequence, is the best qualified to make these ordinances edifying to the Church; while the majority of the elders only rule, visit the sick, superintend Sabbath-schools, conduct prayer-meetings, and make themselves useful in other ways.*

Presbyterians, therefore, maintain a plurality of elders in every church; and as it was in apostolic days, it is customary among them, for elders to rule who do not labor in word and doctrine. Any unprejudiced person may see, from 1 Tim. v. 17, that the office of the eldership divided itself into two great departments of duty in primitive times, even as at present. "Let the elders that rule well be counted worthy of double honor, especially they who labor in word and doctrine." Dr. King's comment on this text must, for sense and truthfulness, commend itself to every intelligent man: "The word," he says, "could suggest to an unbiased reader only one meaning, that all elders who rule well are

* And this distinction in practice is the constitutional law of the Presbyterian Church.   P.

worthy of abundant honor, but especially those of their number who, besides ruling well, also labor in word and doctrine. Of course, the passage so interpreted, bears that, of the elders who rule well, only some labor in word and doctrine—that is, there are ruling elders, and among these teaching elders, as we have at the present day."*

We are tempted thus to insert the true exposition of this celebrated passage, of which we have been often charged by our opponents as giving interpretations the most grotesque and extravagant. But the reader is requested to observe that the point which we have particularly in view at present is that the Presbyterian Church, like the apostolic Church, has in every congregation a plurality of elders.

Office-bearers were set apart to their distinct spheres of duty in the apostolic Church with the laying on of the hands of the presbytery. The Presbyterian Church, in its several branches, is the only one known to us

* Exposition and Defence, p. 115.

that carries this scriptural principle invariably into practice.

In the apostolic Church there was recognized the privilege of appeal and the right of government. This privilege is not only admitted, but it is one of the most distinguishing principles of Presbyterianism. Should any difference arise in a congregation, the members are competent to settle the matter without appeal, if they please; but should this fail, it is equally competent for them to refer the whole matter, either for advice or decision, to the assembly of elders met in presbytery. The highest ecclesiastical court known to the system is the *Presbytery,* the *Synod* being the name usually given to the presbytery of a province, and the *General Assembly* being the name that convenience has attached to the presbytery of a nation. The General Assembly has jurisdiction over a synod only because it is a larger presbytery.*

---

* "The Presbyterian doctrine on this subject is that the Church is one in such a sense that a smaller part is subject to a larger, and the larger to the whole." The elders are the representatives, in the session, of the peo-

APPLICATION OF THE TEST. 115

In the apostolic Church the Lord Jesus alone was King and Head. This is a truth acple of their particular Church. If all Christians could be united in one congregation, nothing further would be necessary. But as they increase in number, and extend territorially, they must have separate organizations; and their unity can be exhibited and kept up only by representation in those organizations, each lower fraction being represented in the higher, and the highest being the bond of unity of all. And as a historical Presbyterian fact, the highest representative body in each country, above the sessions, was first formed as the unit and representative of the whole Church, and out of itself, as the numerical and territorial necessity grew up, it constituted the subordinate organizations. This was the case in Scotland, Ireland and America. The General Assembly is the largest or General Presbytery; and representation is an essential to it.

As against independency or congregationalism, on the one hand, and prelacy on the other, with all the mixtures of the two, the grand distinguishing features of Presbyterianism are the parity of its ministry and representation. Representation again assumes a twofold aspect: 1. In the administration of the government and discipline of each particular church, not by the brethren at large, but by their representatives, elders elected by them and properly ordained; and 2. The representation of these particular congregations through their elders, teaching and ruling, in an ascending grade of church courts, the lower being subject to the higher, knowledged by all Presbyterians, and practically acted upon by all, except a very few, who, owing to their connection with the State, have been charged with a virtual departure from the principle. All Presbyterian churches rank among their most cherished, as well as distinctive, principles, that *Christ alone is King and Head of his Church.* As a denomination, Presbyterians have ever held that the Church, independent of the civil rulers, has supreme jurisdiction in all spiritual matters, and that its office-bearers are bound to exercise that jurisdiction in conformity to the mind of Christ, as expressed in his word. The doctrine of the supreme Headship of Jesus Christ over his Church is one to which Presbyterians have always been warm in their attachment.

We find, then, on minute and patient examination, that the six main principles of government that were, by inspired men, established in the apostolic Church, are all recognized and carried out among Presbyter-

to whom the government of the Church in its more extended territorial capacity is committed.   P.

APPLICATION OF THE TEST. 117

ians. We know no other denomination in the world of whose form of ecclesiastical government the same statement could be made without departure from the truth.

THE RESULT.

Here, then, is the result of our investigations and comparisons. The word of God contains six great, well-defined principles of government that were embodied in that Church which was planted and organized by the inspired apostles of the Lord. All existing modern Churches claim to be apostolic, and, with the exception of the Greek and Roman Churches, profess to adopt the Scriptures as the sole rule of faith and practice. But on comparing the prelacy of the Church of England with the standard of the divine word, it is found that in that Church not one of the apostolic principles of government is recognized or embodied.* Among the inde-

---

* In reference to American Episcopacy this remark must be modified according to the statements on p. 47.

P.

pendents three of the apostolic principles are exemplified in practice; the remaining three are nowhere to be found. Among Presbyterians these six principles are all acknowledged, and every one of them is a main feature of the Presbyterian system. We now remind the reader of the axiom with which we entered on the investigation: *The modern Church which embodies in its government most apostolic principles comes nearest in its government to the apostolic Church.* We apply this axiom to the settlement of the case. Our conclusion is that, *while the prelacy of Rome and England is in direct opposition to the form of ecclesiastical government that was sanctioned by inspired men, and while independency approaches much more nearly, but still falls short of, the primitive model,* THE PRESBYTERIAN IS, IN POINT OF GOVERNMENT, THE ONLY APOSTOLIC CHURCH.

We are, indeed, very far from maintaining that any Church on earth is *in everything* an exact model of the pattern presented in the primitive age. It requires very little thought to see that the apostolic Church of the Scriptures is altogether unique—one that in *all its parts* is never to be realized in this world again. There were in it apostles, prophets and apostolic delegates, all vested with extraordinary powers which have been handed down to no successors. It was quite common for the early preachers to work miracles in confirmation of their doctrine, and confer the Holy Ghost by the laying on of their hands. Sometimes in the same congregation there were several gifted brethren who could look into the future with prophetic eye and declare infallibly the mind of God. There were no public buildings erected for the celebration of Christian worship during all the apostolic age; and public teachers, instead of confining the labors of a life to one little district in the country, went everywhere preaching the word. These are matters as to which no sect that we know of has been able yet to copy the apostolic Church, or is ever very likely to do so.

It is not uncommon to hear people speak of the advantages that accrue to the Presbyterian system from the admittance of the *lay* element into the church courts. This must be a misunderstanding altogether. None but elders—teaching and ruling elders—are competent to sit in any Presbyterian church court, from the session of a congregation up to the General Assembly; and as we have already seen, all elders are equal in point of official standing, for though their departments of duty are in some respects different, yet the office is one and the same. No elder of any kind is a *layman*, but an ecclesiastical officebearer, ordained with the laying on of the hands of the presbytery, and appointed to the oversight of the flock and to the discharge of spiritual duties. The notion is only plausible from the fact that most elders are engaged in secular pursuits. But it should be remembered that all ministers were so engaged at the first. Even an apostle lived by his trade, as he repeatedly informs us (Acts xx. 34; xviii. 3; 1 Cor. iv. 12; 1 Thess. ii. 9; 2 Thess. iii. 8); and it was part of Paul's charge to the bishops of Ephesus, "that *so laboring* they ought to support the weak." Acts xx. 35. If the pursuit of secular employment proves our elders to be laymen, then the bishops of

Ephesus were laymen, and the apostle of the Gentiles was a layman too.

It is, however, only candid to say that such a notion of ecclesiastical order as this term betrays has received countenance from the disparity that in the course of time has risen between the elders who teach and the elders who rule. This disparity is not the result of any ecclesiastical enactment, but was at the beginning, and still is, the effect mainly of a difference of gifts. The most gifted of the elders was in the beginning set to preach, and what at first was only a difference of gifts has grown in the progress of time to wear the appearance of a difference in rank. One is here reminded of the truthful remark of Dr. Campbell: "Power has a sort of attractive force which gives it a tendency to accumulate, insomuch that what in the beginning is a distinction barely perceptible grows in process of time a most remarkable disparity."

The disparity existing between teaching and ruling elders among Presbyterians, instead of being defended, is very much to be lamented, and ought as much as possible to be removed.

This is to be done, however, not by lowering the teaching elder, but by elevating the ruling elder, and appointing to office those only who are distinguished from the people by more than a common measure of graces and gifts, who are aware of the responsibilities of the eldership, and who are determined, for the Lord's sake, to the best of their ability to discharge its duties. Besides, the office of the deacon, existing at present only in some congregations, should be revived in every church where elders can manage temporal matters only by neglecting the spiritual concerns peculiarly their own. These and other defects can be remedied when once they are seen to be defects, for it is one among the many recommendations of the Presbyterian Church polity that it possesses within itself a purifying and reforming power by which, while always preserving the scriptural and essential principles of the system, it can alter any arrangement that experience has proved in its operation not to be productive of good.

We do not, then, assert that the Presbyterian Church is in everything an exact copy of the apostolic Church. There are some things found in the one that must be for ever wanting in the other; and, conversely, there are some things wanting in the one that are found in the other. But in doctrine they are exactly the same; in worship they are exactly the same; in government all the main principles of the one are found in the other. There is no other Church on earth of which the same statements can be made in truth. We regard it, therefore, as put beyond all reasonable doubt *that of all the Churches now existing in the world, the Presbyterian Church comes nearest to the model of apostolic times.* That such is the fact every man who gives to the evidence here submitted that careful and unprejudiced consideration to which it is entitled must, as we think, be convinced.

www.ingramcontent.com/pod-product-compliance
Lightning Source LLC
Chambersburg PA
CBHW021941160426
43195CB00011B/1183